SCHOLASTIC
READ & RESPOND

Bringing the best books to life in the classroom

Activities based on

The Highway Rat

By Julia Donaldson
& Axel Scheffler

The Highway Rat

JULIA DONALDSON · AXEL SCHEFFLER

FOR AGES 5–7

Scholastic Education, an imprint of Scholastic Ltd
Book End, Range Road, Witney, Oxfordshire, OX29 0YD
Registered office: Westfield Road, Southam, Warwickshire CV47 0RA

Printed and bound by Ashford Colour Press
© 2018 Scholastic Ltd
1 2 3 4 5 6 7 8 9   8 9 0 1 2 3 4 5 6 7

British Library Cataloguing-in-Publication Data
A catalogue record for this book is available from the British Library.
ISBN 978-1407-18254-4

Extracts from *The National Curriculum in England, English Programme of Study* © Crown Copyright. Reproduced under the terms of the Open Government Licence (OGL). http://www.nationalarchives.gov.uk/doc/open-government-licence/version/3

Due to the nature of the web, we cannot guarantee the content or links of any site mentioned. We strongly recommend that teachers check websites before using them in the classroom.

Author Jean Evans
Editorial team Rachel Morgan, Vicki Yates, Suzanne Adams, Julia Roberts
Series designers Neil Salt and Alice Duggan
Designer Alice Duggan
Illustrator Dave Smith/Beehive Illustration

Acknowledgements
The publishers gratefully acknowledge permission to reproduce the following copyright material: **Scholastic UK** for the use of the Extract and illustrations from *The Highway Rat* by Julia Donaldson and Axel Scheffler, text copyright © 2011 Julia Donaldson, illustrations copyright © Axel Scheffler (2011, Alison Green Books).
Every effort has been made to trace copyright holders for the works reproduced in this book, and the publishers apologise for any inadvertent omissions.

CONTENTS ▼

How to use Read & Respond in your classroom...

Read & Respond provides teaching ideas related to a specific well-loved children's book. Each Read & Respond book is divided into the following sections:

ABOUT THE BOOK AND AUTHOR

Gives you some background information about the book and the author.

GUIDED READING

Breaks the book down into sections and gives notes for using it with guided reading groups. A bookmark has been provided on page 10 containing comprehension questions. The children can be directed to refer to these as they read.

SHARED READING

Provides extracts from the children's book with associated notes for focused work. There is also one non-fiction extract that relates to the children's book.

PHONICS & SPELLING

Provides word-level work related to the children's book so you can teach phonics and spelling in context.

PLOT, CHARACTER & SETTING

Contains activity ideas focused on the plot, characters and the setting of the story.

PLOT, CHARACTER & SETTING

Tell the story

• Cut out the boxes and arrange the sentences in order to tell the story.

Some ants crawled by with a leaf. The Highway Rat took it.

A duck came waddling along. The Highway Rat wanted to eat her.

At last, the Highway Rat found a way out of the cave.

The Highway Rat was a baddie and a beast.

A squirrel bounded past with some nuts. The Highway Rat took them.

The Highway Rat found a job in a cake shop.

A rabbit hopped by with some clover. The Highway Rat took it.

The duck led the Highway Rat into a cave to look for her sister.

GET WRITING

Provides writing activities related to the children's book. These activities may be based directly on the children's book or be broadly based on the themes and concepts of the story.

TALK ABOUT IT

Has speaking and listening activities related to the children's book. These activities may be based directly on the children's book or be broadly based on the themes and concepts of the story.

ASSESSMENT

Contains short activities that will help you assess whether the children have understood concepts and curriculum objectives. They are designed to be informal activities to feed into your planning.

Activities

The activities follow the same format:

- **Objective:** the objective for the lesson. It will be based upon a curriculum objective, but will often be more specific to the focus being covered.

- **What you need:** a list of resources you need to teach the lesson, including photocopiable pages.

- **What to do:** the activity notes.

- **Differentiation:** this is provided where specific and useful differentiation advice can be given to support and/or extend the learning in the activity.

The activities are numbered for reference within each section and should move through the text sequentially – so you can use the lesson while you are reading the book. Once you have read the book, most of the activities can be used in any order you wish.

> **❝** The titles are great fun to use and cover exactly the range of books that children most want to read. It makes it easy to explore texts fully and ensure the children want to keep on reading more. **❞**
>
> *Chris Flanagan, Year 5 Teacher, St Thomas of Canterbury Primary School*

Section	Activity	Curriculum objectives
Guided reading		Comprehension: To participate in discussion about books...that are read to them, taking turns and listening to what others say; to explain clearly their understanding of what is read to them.
Shared reading	1	Comprehension: To participate in discussion about what is read to them, taking turns and listening to what others say; to explain clearly their understanding of what is read to them.
	2	Comprehension: To recognise simple recurring literary language in stories and poetry.
	3	Comprehension: To listen to and discuss... non-fiction at a level beyond that at which they can read independently. Word reading: To apply phonic knowledge and skills as the route to decode words.
Phonics & spelling	1	Spelling: To write from memory simple sentences dictated by the teacher...
	2	Word reading: To read words with contractions... and understand that the apostrophe represents the omitted letter(s).
	3	Spelling: To use the spelling rules for adding 's' or 'es'.
	4	Word reading: To read words of more than one syllable that contain taught GPCs.
Plot, character & setting	1	Comprehension: To discuss the sequence of events in books...
	2	Spoken language: To participate in discussions, presentations, performances, role play, improvisations and debates.
	3	Comprehension: To make inferences on the basis of what is being said and done.
	4	Comprehension: To draw on what they already know or on background information and vocabulary provided by the teacher.
	5	Comprehension: To listen to and discuss a wide range of poems, stories and non-fiction....
	6	Comprehension: To recognise and join in with predictable phrases.
Talk about it	1	Spoken language: To maintain attention and participate actively in collaborative conversations... responding to comments. Spelling: To name the letters of the alphabet in order.
	2	Spoken language: To gain, maintain and monitor the interest of the listener(s).
	3	Spoken language: To articulate and justify answers, arguments and opinions. Word reading: To apply phonic knowledge and skills as the route to decode words.
	4	Spoken language: To articulate and justify answers, arguments and opinions.
	5	Spoken language: To listen and respond appropriately to adults and their peers.
	6	Spoken language: To develop understanding through speculating, hypothesising, imagining and exploring ideas.
Get writing	1	Vocabulary, grammar and punctuation: To begin to punctuate sentences using a capital letter and a full stop, question mark or exclamation mark.
	2	Spelling: To spell the days of the week.
	3	Composition: To sequence sentences to form short narratives.
	4	Composition: To read aloud their writing clearly enough to be heard...
	5	Composition: To sequence sentences to form short narratives.
	6	Composition: To discuss what they have written with the teacher or other pupils; to write for different purposes.
Assessment	1	Comprehension: To become very familiar with key stories, fairy stories and traditional tales, retelling them and considering their particular characteristics.
	2	Vocabulary, grammar and punctuation: To use the grammatical terminology in English Appendix 2 in discussing their writing.
	3	Composition: To write sentences by re-reading what they have written to check that it makes sense.
	4	Composition: To compose a sentence orally before writing it.

About the book

Julia Donaldson has based *The Highway Rat* on Alfred Noyes' well-loved poem, 'The Highwayman'. It tells the story of a greedy rat riding through the countryside searching for animal travellers to steal from. He certainly lives up to his reputation as a 'baddie' and a 'beast' as he viciously robs the creatures of their food whether or not he really wants it. Children will surely empathise with the poor animal victims as they become thinner and thinner. However, all is not lost when a plucky duck lures the rat into a cave by pretending her sister is in there with biscuits and buns. The rat eagerly strides in and wanders in the dark until eventually he emerges at the other side, far, far away. The duck jumps on the rat's horse and gallops back to her hungry friends with the stolen food. The happy animals hold a huge feast with food, music and dancing. As the story draws to a close, children can be encouraged to consider the difference between the good deeds of the duck and the bad deeds of the rat. As always, they will warm to Axel Scheffler's humorous illustrations, and appreciate the effects of the rich, patterned language, rollicking rhyme and satisfying repetition that are so much a part of Julia Donaldson stories.

About the author

Julia Donaldson is one of our most popular children's authors, perhaps most famous for *The Gruffalo*. Her musical background is apparent in the lilting language and strong rhythms that children so enjoy in all of her books. Julia was awarded an MBE for Services to Literature in 2011, and was the seventh Children's Laureate from 2011–2013. Her portrait by Peter Monkman hangs in the National Portrait Gallery.

About the illustrator

Axel Scheffler is a German illustrator of bestselling picture books such as *The Bedtime Bear* and *The Tickle Book*. He has collaborated on picture books with Julia Donaldson since the publication of *A Squash and a Squeeze* in 1993. His quirky characters, with their distinctive features and humorous details, abound on every page to enhance Julia Donaldson's unique and wonderful verse. Other popular books published by this successful partnership include *The Gruffalo*, *The Gruffalo's Child*, *Tiddler*, *Stick Man* and *Tabby McTat*.

Key facts

The Highway Rat

⦿ **Author:**
Julia Donaldson

⦿ **Illustrator:**
Axel Scheffler

⦿ **First published:**
2011 by Alison Green Books

⦿ **Awards:**
Julia and Axel's books have won many awards, including the Smarties Book Prize and the British Book Awards Children's Book of the Year (twice).

⦿ **Did you know?**
A BBC animated version of *The Highway Rat* was televised on Christmas Day 2017. *The Reiver Rat* is a version of *The Highway Rat* written in Scots dialect.

GUIDED READING ▶

Cover story

Explore the illustrations and text on the front and back covers of the book together before predicting the possible story content. Read the title and ask question 1 on the Guided reading bookmark. Establish that the story is likely to be about a highway rat and, if necessary, explain the meaning of 'highway' in this context.

Draw attention to the names Julia Donaldson and Axel Scheffler, establishing which one is the author and which one the illustrator. (You could use the information on page 7 to extend this discussion.) Invite children to share memories of books by this author and illustrator pairing and what they recall about their distinctive styles (for example, catchy repetition and rhyme, and funny characters with large eyes). Ask question 4 on the bookmark, and identify Axel Scheffler's distinctive style on the facial expressions of the animals.

Following this cover exploration, encourage children to voice their initial expectations about the likely style and content of the book.

Top tips

As you read the book for the first time, try to build upon the initial impressions you formed together after exploring the cover. Pronounce words clearly and use appropriate expression, encouraging children to join in when words are repeated. Pause slightly before words that conclude rhyming couplets so that children can anticipate what they are and appreciate the author's satisfying word choice. Engage children by adopting varied and consistent contrast between the menacing tones of the Highway Rat, the timid voices of the animals he is robbing, and the persuasive charm of the plucky duck. Use clues from the text to indicate how the Highway Rat might sound, for example, when the Highway Rat 'thundered', 'snarled', 'bellowed' and 'complained'. Vary the volume as you imitate the diminishing echoing sounds coming from the cave. Introduce appropriate body movements, such as adopting the stance of a sword fighter holding an imaginary sword aloft as indicated by the illustrations, and change your facial expressions to contrast the feelings of the greedy rat and the frightened, sad animals. Pause for effect when indicated by an ellipsis, and stop at significant points to ask what might happen next or to predict a word or phrase, for example, after reading the words 'I am… (…the Rat of the Highway)'.

Divide initial reading into four sections, focusing on different aspects of the story.

Spreads 1–3

As you read this first section, encourage children to voice their understanding of the meaning of the text through appropriate comments and queries. For instance, ask question 2 on the bookmark to establish what kind of character the Highway Rat might be. Extend the discussion if necessary to talk about the actions of 'goodies' and 'baddies' in stories the children have read. Focus on the words the author uses to describe the Highway Rat's manners ('rough', 'rude'). Ask question 6 on the bookmark, and invite children to contrast how they think people with good and bad manners might behave. Decide which category the Highway Rat falls into. Discuss how effective descriptive words help us to establish 'mind's eye' images, for example, the Highway Rat's 'sharp', 'yellow' teeth and his 'scornful' look. Comment together on how the text and illustrations work in unison to create these 'mind's eye' images.

Spreads 4–7

As you read this section, focus on how the phrase that first appeared in the previous section, 'I am the Rat of the Highway', becomes established as it is repeated a further six times. Read the whole section, inviting the children to chant this phrase as you keep silent. Speculate that this phrase might occur in later sections. Talk about how satisfying it is to enjoy repetition in a story. Discuss the meaning of vocabulary that is possibly new, such as 'bounding', extending understanding by encouraging a few children to demonstrate this movement. Explain the meaning of words, such as 'reining' and 'éclairs', and the phrase 'Stand and deliver!' in this context. Reinforce understanding of 'snarled' by encouraging children to repeat the words of The Highway Rat, 'I'll have no ifs or buts!', in a snarling way.

Discuss how the rich and detailed illustrations enhance the story: explore the expressions and movement of the characters in the small illustrations alongside the short sentences in spread 7 and talk about the additional information they convey. Ask question 5 on the bookmark.

Spreads 8–11

As you read through this section, invite children to consider how the direction of the story changes when the duck is introduced. Ask question 8 on the bookmark and discuss what happened to the Highway Rat and how the duck deceived him. Ask the children if they think the duck's sister is really in the cave and to give reasons for their answers. Based on this discussion, ask children to predict what might happen in the next section. Ask question 3 on the bookmark and explore how the differing size of the lettering is used to denote the diminishing sound of the echo in the cave.

Spend time focusing on the element of rhyme. Read through each page of the section again, identifying the rhyming pairs of words together. Try repeating each pair as a chant, clapping as you do so, for example, 'end/bend, end/bend'. Ask question 7 on the bookmark and discuss the importance of this feature in relation to the story read so far. Ask whether the children think the rest of the book will follow the same pattern. Try substituting rhyming words with non-rhyming words that have similar meanings, for example, 'end/bend', 'finish/bend'. Ask which version had rhyming words and decide together which one sounds best. Always be prepared to follow the children's comments, interests and ideas as you talk, and encourage respect for differing opinions.

Spreads 12–15

When reading this final section, ask about whether the children's predictions were correct. Explore the illustration on the last spread, and focus on the expressions of the characters. Look at each one in turn and discuss what they are doing or saying. Ask: *What do you think the wolf is saying to the sheep behind the counter? What is the girl wolf asking? What is the cat peering through the door thinking? What is the Highway Rat doing? Why has he got his back to the others?* Explore the rat's expression in particular and compare this to those of the other characters. Talk about how he now has to eat the scraps he has swept off the floor instead of taking anything he wants from the other animals. Ask question 10 on the bookmark.

Discuss the ending and ask whether they think it is a good or bad one, and encourage them to give reasons for their answers. What do they think will happen to the Highway Rat next? Discuss the important message the book contains, for example, ask: *Should we take things from others without their permission? Why is it wrong to steal from others?*

After exploring the book section by section, ask question 9 on the bookmark to encourage the children to reconsider their initial impressions.

The Highway Rat

by Julia Donaldson & Axel Scheffler

Focus on... Meaning

1. Who do you think the Highway Rat is? Does the title provide any clues about the story?

2. What do you think the words 'baddie' and 'beast' tell us about the character of the Highway Rat?

Focus on... Organisation

3. How does the author use letter size to show that there is an echo in the cave?

4. Why do you think Axel Scheffler's illustrations are easy to recognise? What do you like/dislike about them?

5. How do you think the small, detailed illustrations alongside the words help us to understand more about the feelings of the characters?

■SCHOLASTIC
READ & RESPOND
Bringing the best books to life in the classroom

The Highway Rat

by Julia Donaldson & Axel Scheffler

Focus on... Language and features

6. How do you think the Highway Rat might behave if his manners are rough and rude?

7. Describe the rhyme pattern. Do you think writing in rhyme is effective in this story?

Focus on... Purpose, viewpoints and effects

8. How does the duck avoid being eaten? Think of words to describe the duck's character.

9. Do you think your initial impressions of the book have changed? Why do you think this?

10. After exploring the last illustration, do you think the rat has changed by the end of the story? What makes you think this?

■SCHOLASTIC
READ & RESPOND
Bringing the best books to life in the classroom

SHARED READING ▶

Extract 1

- Display and read an enlarged copy of Extract 1. Explain that these are the opening lines of the story. Invite children to circle the name of the main character ('The Highway Rat') and words that give information about his character. Ask: *What do we know about the main character after reading these opening lines?*

- Highlight the rhyming words and suggest that the text resembles a poem.

- Identify the letters used to form the 'ee' sound in the words 'feast' and 'beast' together ('ea') and think of other words with the same digraph creating the same sound ('treat', 'beat'). Find a word with the letters 'ee' for the 'ee' sound and highlight this ('teeth'). Ask: *How is the 'oo' sound created in the rhyming words 'rude' and 'food'?*

- Explore the rhythm created by the repetition of 'riding' and suggest that this might resemble the sound of the hooves of a galloping horse.

Extract 2

- Display and read an enlarged copy of Extract 2, explaining that these are the closing lines of the story. Ask: *Do you think this is a good ending to this story? Why do you think this? Which adjectives describe the appearance of the Highway Rat? How has he changed since the story began? Has he changed for better or worse? What makes you think this?*

- Recall the repetition of the word 'riding' in Extract 1. Now highlight the words 'cake shop' and count the times they appear. Ask: *How do you think repeating the words 'cake shop' improves this extract?*

- Underline the ellipsis and ask why it is there. Read the extract with and without a pause. Ask: *Why do you think the author wants the reader to pause at this point?* (to show time passing)

- Discuss the meaning of the word 'echoey' and ask the children to think of other words to describe the cave.

Extract 3

- Explain that you are going to show the children a factsheet about highwaymen and invite them to speculate about what might be included. Discuss the difference between fiction and non-fiction, and ask which category a factsheet belongs in. Ask: *Why do you think we need factsheets?*

- Display an enlarged copy of Extract 3 and draw their attention to the useful words in bold. Ask children to read the first sentence, encouraging them to tackle longer, unfamiliar words by reading each syllable separately before combining them to read the whole word. Provide support with words that still challenge them.

- Read and discuss the meaning of the rest of the sentences.

- Ask questions to establish children's understanding of what has been read, such as: *Why did highwaymen carry pistols? Can you describe a tricorn hat?*

- Finally, ask the children to make up sentences using the useful words in the box at the bottom of the page. Explain that these words might be useful for future writing about highwaymen.

Extract 1

The Highway Rat was a baddie.

The Highway Rat was a beast.

He took what he wanted and ate what he took.

His life was one long feast.

His teeth were sharp and yellow,

his manners were rough and rude,

And the Highway Rat went riding –

Riding – riding –

Riding along the highway

and stealing the travellers' food.

Extract 2

And as for the Rat in the echoey cave,

    he shouted and wandered, till...

He found his way out of the darkness,

    on the other side of the hill.

A thinner and greyer and meeker Rat,

    he robs on the road no more,

For he landed a job in a cake shop –

    A cake shop – a cake shop –

And they say he still works in the cake shop,

    sweeping the cake shop floor.

Extract 3

Highwaymen attacked **travellers** and stole things like jewels and money. Highwaymen sometimes **robbed** alone and sometimes in **gangs**.

Highwaymen normally rode horses and carried **pistols**.

Highwaymen usually wore **tricorn** hats, black clothes, high boots, and eye **masks** to hide their faces.
A **tricorn** hat has three corners.

Highwaymen often robbed **stagecoaches**.
A stagecoach is a carriage pulled by horses.

"Stand and deliver" were famous words used by highwaymen.

Dick Turpin was a famous **highwayman** who lived over two hundred years ago.

Useful words

highwayman

robber

gang

pistol

stagecoach

traveller

tricorn

mask

PHONICS & SPELLING ▶

1. Listen and write

Objective
To write from memory simple sentences dictated by the teacher that include words using the GPCs and common exception words taught so far.

What you need
Prepared sentences for dictation, individual whiteboards.

What to do

- Make sure that your prepared sentences include examples of GPCs and common exception words taught so far, for example, 'Once there was a wicked rat who liked to steal food./The thief stole a green leaf from the ants./The rat grew fatter and fatter after eating so much food.' (Common exception words are in italic.)

- Discuss how some words are more difficult to spell because they do not follow the rules the children have been taught. They need to learn these words.

- Remind children that different combinations of letters are often used to represent the same sound. Ask volunteers to write the words 'thief', 'green' and 'leaf' on the board and ask the class to identify the letters used to create the 'ee' sound in each word.

- Explain that you are going to read some sentences one at a time and that you want the children to write them on their whiteboards. Read slowly and carefully.

- Invite the children to exchange their whiteboards with a partner and to read one another's sentences to check that they make sense.

- Finally, write each sentence on the board and allow time for partners to identify errors.

2. Expand and contract

Objective
To read words with contractions, and understand that the apostrophe represents the omitted letter(s).

What you need
Copies of The Highway Rat.

What to do

- Recap what is meant by a contraction by writing sentences from The Highway Rat on the board, for example, 'In that case, I'll have to eat you!' and 'I doubt if you're terribly juicy.' Identify the contractions and circle them. Talk about which words have been shortened ('will' and 'are').

- Explain that we often use contractions when we speak, and give examples, such as 'If it's sunny later we'll go outside.' Identify the contracted words.

- Read aloud the page containing the duck's words from 'Hang on,' to '...eat your fill.' once with and once without the contractions. Decide together when and why the rhythm changes. Suggest that Julia Donaldson sometimes contracts her chosen words to make the rhyme and rhythm flow.

- Revise, or explain, the difference between an apostrophe used to denote possession and one that is used in a contraction, for example, 'The Highway Rat's teeth are sharp.' versus 'The Highway Rat's a baddie.' Ask children which sentence contains the contraction. Try saying the first sentence as if the apostrophe denotes a contraction: 'The Highway Rat is teeth are sharp.' Discuss what is wrong with this sentence.

- Invite children to link the animals in the story with their possessions using an apostrophe, for example, 'rabbit's clover', 'ant's leaf'.

Differentiation
Extension: Encourage children to find contractions in the story and then rewrite the sentences in full, with the contractions removed.

3. Come shopping

Objective
To use the spelling rules for adding 's' or 'es', as listed in English Appendix 1.

What you need
Copies of *The Highway Rat*, art materials.

Cross-curricular link
Art and design

What to do

- Read *The Highway Rat* before focusing on the cake shop illustration on the final spread. Ask these questions to encourage children to explore detail: *Can you describe the cake that the sheep is taking from the glass case? How many Gruffalo biscuits can you count? What is in the sacks on the floor?*

- Draw attention to the wall poster. Suggest that it shows images and names of items sold in the shop to tempt customers to buy them. Explain that you would like children to work with partners to create attractive posters to hang on the shop wall.

- Revise the rule for plural endings before children start working: if the ending sounds like 's' or 'z' it is spelled 's'; if it sounds like 'iz' it is spelled 'es'.

- Write single items on the board and ask the children to put them on their posters in the plural. Items could include: 'strawberry tart', 'crunchy fox', 'chocolate éclair', 'ham sandwich', 'Gruffalo biscuit', 'cheese roll', 'cream bun'.

- Provide access to art materials. Allow time for pairs to finish their posters before sharing them with the class. Discuss correct plural endings.

Differentiation

Support: Ask children to create a poster with plural items ending in 's' initially.

Extension: Challenge children to add the following items in the plural: 'sugar mouse', 'granary loaf', 'gingerbread man', 'Cornish pasty'.

4. Searching for syllables

Objective
To read words of more than one syllable that contain taught GPCs.

What you need
Copies of *The Highway Rat*.

What to do

- Practise breaking words down into separate syllables. Choose words from *The Highway Rat* with one, two and three syllables and write them on the board (for example, 'rat', 'sister', 'deafening'). Revise what a syllable is, explaining that it sounds like a beat in a word. Read the three words on the board and count the syllables together by clapping the beats. Ask: *Which word has three syllables? How do you know?*

- Talk about how some words can be separated into two different words (for example, 'high/way') and are called compound words. Discuss the meaning of 'highway', and of the two words that combine to make it.

- Have fun with words from the book with two syllables, making up chants by clapping or stamping the syllable beats repeatedly (for example, 'riding/highway, yellow/baddie, riding/highway, yellow/baddie').

- Divide the children into groups and suggest having a competition to see which group can make the longest list of words consisting of two syllables from *The Highway Rat* (no word can be listed twice).

- Allow time to complete lists before sharing results with the class. Comment on the more unusual words discovered.

Differentiation

Support: Ask children to concentrate on finding ten words with one or two syllables, depending on reading ability.

Extension: Invite children to list as many three-syllable words as they can in a favourite story.

PLOT, CHARACTER & SETTING ▶

1. Tell the story

Objective
To discuss the sequence of events in books.

What you need
Copies of *The Highway Rat*, photocopiable page 20 'Tell the story'.

What to do

- Read *The Highway Rat* together. Discuss how the first half of the story follows a regular pattern as the Highway Rat stops different animals to steal their food. Identify the point at which this pattern changes (when the duck appears).

- Talk about events after this point, leading to the Highway Rat working in the cake shop.

- Display photocopiable page 20 'Tell the story'. Read the sentences together, asking why the story makes no sense. Discuss the order of the remaining sentences.

- Invite children to complete the photocopiable sheet in pairs.

- When they have finished, and are satisfied that their sentence order tells the story, bring the class together to share results. Choose a few pairs to read their stories and note any differences between them. Agree as a class on the final order.

Differentiation
Support: Ask children to find the two sentences representing the beginning and end of the story.

Extension: Ask children to compose two sentences about what happened when the Highway Rat met the cat and spider, and slot them into the sequence.

2. The rat's journey

Objective
To participate in discussions, presentations, performances, role play, improvisations and debates.

What you need
Copies of *The Highway Rat*, a selection of simple maps, story map resources such as small plastic animals or card images representing story characters, art materials.

Cross-curricular link
Drama

What to do

- Invite children to share their map experiences, for example, exploring an atlas or following a local street plan.

- Discuss how maps are useful when travelling. Recall previous activities involving story maps, or introduce the children to this useful method of sequencing events if they are not already familiar with them.

- Suggest creating story maps of *The Highway Rat* story to help children remember the sequence of events as the rat travels along the road, through the cave and into the cake shop.

- Divide the class into small groups and provide access to story map resources. Encourage the children to draw a road on the back of wallpaper, create a cave from a box and use doll's house furniture for the cake shop. Decorate the map with art materials.

- Once the map is finished, ask children to retell the story as a group, moving small animals along the surface.

Differentiation
Extension: Ask children to perform the story to the class using their story map and the additional resources.

3. Rat detectives

Objective
To make inferences on the basis of what is being said and done.

What you need
Copies of *The Highway Rat*.

What to do
- Read *The Highway Rat* to the children, and establish that the title is also the name of the book's main character.

- Explain that you are pretending to be a police inspector searching for evidence about a highway rat who has been frightening local animals and stealing from them. This evidence can then be used to capture the villain.

- Invite the children to be your detectives in groups, asking each group to keep a factsheet about this rat. Create a demonstration sheet on the board headed 'The Highway Rat' with two sections underneath headed 'Appearance' and 'Character'.

- Provide each group with a copy of the book and a sheet of paper. Ask them to read the book together and make notes under the appropriate heading on the sheet as they go along, with words that describe how the rat looks and behaves ('sharp yellow teeth' and 'rough rude manners'). Include under 'Appearance' word clues linked to the illustrations, such as 'tricorn hat', 'boots', 'mask' and 'sword'.

- Hold a 'detective meeting' with all groups to share factsheets, using the words 'assume' and 'infer' as you talk to them. Explain that we do this when we form an impression of a character from their actions and behaviour, for example: *We assume/ We can infer that the rat is cruel because of the way he takes everything from the hungry animals even if it is something he dislikes.*

4. Making comparisons (1)

Objective
To draw on what they already know or on background information and vocabulary provided by the teacher.

What you need
Copies of *The Highway Rat*; highwaymen images from websites and other sources; drawing, painting and simple collage resources, such as tissue paper, wool and sequins.

Cross-curricular link
Art and design

What to do
- Read *The Highway Rat* aloud, holding up the pages to refresh children's memories of the main character's appearance. Show some highwaymen images on a large screen if possible and ask the children to describe how the story character is similar in appearance to these images. Now invite them to highlight any differences in appearances.

- Suggest that the children work in pairs to create a large picture of a highwayman standing next to the Highway Rat. Provide them with access to copies of the book and images of highwaymen, either printed or on screen.

- Ask them to use the materials provided to make an interesting picture that reflects the similarities and differences between the two characters.

- Encourage children to discuss labels they could include and where they might put them, for example, they may put labels reflecting similarities down the centre and draw a line to join them to each character, and labels that reflect differences down the edge linked to the relevant character by lines. Ask children to add the labels to their pictures.

- Bring the class together and invite a few of the pairs to share their completed pictures and talk through similarities and differences highlighted. Praise interesting and unusual similarities and differences.

5. Making comparisons (2)

Objective

To listen to and discuss a wide range of poems, stories and non-fiction at a level beyond that at which they can read independently.

What you need

Copies of The Highway Rat, children's artwork from 'Making comparisons (1)', photocopiable page 21 'Making comparisons', Extract 3.

Cross-curricular link

History

What to do

- Recall together highwayman facts from Extract 3, and the children's pictorial comparisons from Activity 4. Display and read Extract 3 together, revising why it is a non-fiction sheet.

- Now display photocopiable page 21 'Making comparisons'. Read the bold sentences together, establishing that these are true facts.

- Explain that the children are going to complete the sentences underneath the factual ones, to highlight similarities and differences between the two. Read the first sentence and ask: *Did the Highway Rat also steal things from travellers?* Clarify that the sentence should be completed to reflect this similarity. Read the second sentence and ask: *What is different about the Highway Rat?* (sword not pistol, rat not man) Discuss ways to complete this sentence. Revise differences between fiction and non-fiction before discussing how to complete the next sentence. Clarify the meaning of 'gang' before discussing completion of the final sentence.

- Provide each child with the photocopiable sheet to complete. Display Extract 3, and provide their artwork from the previous activity and copies of *The Highway Rat* for reference.

- Bring the class together to share their completed photocopiable sheets and artwork.

Differentiation

Support: Suggest children complete as many sentences as they can, giving support when necessary.

6. Exploring the setting

Objective

To recognise and join in with predictable phrases.

What you need

Copies of The Highway Rat, dictionary, individual whiteboards.

What to do

- Recall previous discussions about story settings. Establish that there are three different settings in *The Highway Rat* – the highway, the cave and the cake shop – but that most of the events take place along the highway.

- Read a simple dictionary definition of a highway. Establish that it is usually a major road connecting two big towns, but that the word can also refer to any public track. Discuss the sort of highway that is the setting for much of *The Highway Rat* (a countryside track).

- Ask the children to imagine they are walking along the highway and to think of what they might see (excluding story characters), for example, mountains, rocks, stones, trees, flowers. Explore the book's illustrations to help.

- Divide children into groups to discuss and write a list of 'setting' words associated with the highway.

- Recall the memory game 'I went to the market and I bought a…', where individuals add to the list until it becomes too long to remember. Suggest playing 'I walked along the highway and I saw…', with each group choosing one word from their whiteboard to add. When a group fails to remember the accumulated lists they must stop playing. Praise the group who remember the most.

Differentiation

Extension: Extend the game to include 'I crept into the cave and I saw…' or 'I went to the cake shop and I bought…'.

Tell the story

- Cut out the boxes and arrange the sentences in order to tell the story.

Some ants crawled by with a leaf. The Highway Rat took it.	
A duck came waddling along. The Highway Rat wanted to eat her.	
At last, the Highway Rat found a way out of the cave.	
The Highway Rat was a baddie and a beast.	
A squirrel bounded past with some nuts. The Highway Rat took them.	
The Highway Rat found a job in a cake shop.	
A rabbit hopped by with some clover. The Highway Rat took it.	
The duck led the Highway Rat into a cave to look for her sister.	

Making comparisons

- Read the sentences about highwaymen, then finish the incomplete sentences about the Highway Rat.

1. A highwayman stole things from travellers.

The Highway Rat _____

_____

2. A highwayman rode a horse and carried a pistol.

The Highway Rat _____

_____

3. Dick Turpin was a real highwayman.

The Highway Rat _____

_____

4. A highwayman often wore a tricorn hat, boots and a mask.

The Highway Rat _____

_____

5. A highwayman sometimes robbed with others in a gang.

The Highway Rat _____

_____

TALK ABOUT IT ▶

1. Alphabetical order

Objective
Maintain attention and participate actively in collaborative conversations... responding to comments; to name the letters of the alphabet in alphabetical order.

What you need
Children's dictionaries; alphabet chart; five large cards, with words 'rat', 'rabbit', 'squirrel', 'ant', 'duck'; sets of five cards for each group depicting the names of five different animals.

What to do
- Ask children when they might use a dictionary. Talk about how the words are arranged in alphabetical order.

- Ask questions about the letters on an alphabet chart, for example, *Which letter comes first/last/before 'm'?* Make sure that children use the correct letter names when answering.

- Hold up the large cards, read the names on them together. Explain that you would like the children to arrange these cards in alphabetical order. Encourage discussion about the order of the names 'rabbit' and 'rat'.

- Divide the children into groups of five; each with a set of animal cards to arrange in alphabetical order. Suggest that they choose a card each and arrange themselves in a line holding the cards in alphabetical order in front of them. Encourage discussion amongst group members about the order they stand in.

Differentiation
Support: Make sure names start with different letters.

Extension: Include extra animal names in the card set and ensure a number of them start with the same letter.

2. Aspiring actors

Objective
To gain, maintain and monitor the interest of the listener(s).

What you need
Copies of *The Highway Rat*; enough animal name cards to divide equally between two halves of the class.

Cross-curricular link
Drama

What to do
- Read *The Highway Rat*, focusing on the interactions between the rat and the animals he meets along the highway.

- Discuss how the rat's voice might sound (for example, loud/quiet, rough/smooth, kind/unkind, frightening/calming). Invite individuals to demonstrate how they imagine the rat's voice sounds by repeating 'Who goes there?' using different voices.

- Briefly consider the voices of the other main characters, using the book for ideas. Point out that the squirrel stopped 'with a shake and a shiver' and ask: *Would this affect his voice?*

- Explain that you would like children to work in pairs and dramatise a short scene between the rat and another character. Divide into pairs, asking them to play the rat's encounter with the character named on the card pulled from a box.

- Interact with the children as they practise their scenes. Encourage them to consider body language, interesting voices and imaginative vocabulary.

- Bring the class together to watch and comment on the re-enactments. Invite them to choose the most engaging scene between the rat and the rabbit, squirrel, ant or duck.

- Put the chosen scenes in order together and perform the entire story to another class.

3. Contrasting characters

Objective

To articulate and justify answers, arguments and opinions; to apply phonic knowledge and skills as the route to decode words.

What you need

Copies of *The Highway Rat*, photocopiable page 25 'Contrasting characters'.

Cross-curricular link

PSHE

What to do

- Ask children to recall good and bad characters in books they have read, and what they liked or disliked about them. Decide together on contrasting qualities and actions associated with good and bad characters.

- Explore the characters of the rat and the duck in *The Highway Rat*. Ask: *What sort of characters do you think the rat and the duck are? Why do you think this?*

- Display an enlarged version of photocopiable page 25 'Contrasting characters'. Invite the children to read the words in the boxes. Explain that half of these words describe the Highway Rat and half describe the duck.

- Discuss the meaning of each word together, encouraging the children to use their phonic knowledge and skills to decode them. For example, point out the split vowel digraphs ('u–e') in the word 'rude' and discuss how they change the 'u' into an 'oo' sound or compare the vowel digraphs used to create the /ee/ phoneme in the words 'beast' and 'plucky'.

- Divide the class into pairs and provide each child with the photocopiable sheet to complete. Encourage the children to read the words in the boxes out loud and to talk about which character they describe before filling in the page individually.

- Bring the class together to share their work.

Differentiation

Extension: Challenge children to think of their own words to describe each character. Encourage them to talk about the reasons for their choice with their partner before writing the words under their pictures.

4. Conscience alley

Objective

To articulate and justify answers, arguments and opinions.

What you need

Copies of *The Highway Rat*.

Cross-curricular link

PSHE

What to do

- Read *The Highway Rat* and discuss the main character's actions. Ask: *Do you think the Highway Rat was right to take the animals' food? Why/why not?*

- Now consider the actions of the duck together. Ask: *Was the duck right to trick the rat? Why/why not?*

- Discuss occasions when the children have been upset after someone has taken something from them. Who helped to make them feel better and how?

- Divide into groups to discuss the importance of sharing and why it is wrong to steal. Briefly share group responses as a class.

- Recall previous experiences of 'conscience alley' activities, or explain how such activities can help someone to decide what to do when faced with a dilemma. Suggest that the children use this method to encourage the Highway Rat to realise that it is wrong to steal.

- Divide into two groups in the roles of highwaymen/women and animal characters. Invite the highwaymen/women to think of reasons why they steal, and the animals to consider why they think stealing is wrong.

- Form two lines down the centre of the hall (highwaymen/women and animals). Choose someone to play the part of the Highway Rat walking slowly between the lines listening to arguments for and against stealing.

- Invite the Highway Rat to tell everyone whether he will continue to steal, or think again about stealing, after considering their arguments. Repeat with different children playing the Highway Rat.

5. Hot-seat interviews

Objective

To listen and respond appropriately to adults and their peers.

What you need

Copies of *The Highway Rat*, individual cards depicting character names (rabbit, squirrel, ant, cat, spider, horse, duck, Highway Rat), individual whiteboards.

Cross-curricular link

PSHE

What to do

- Read *The Highway Rat* before focusing on the spread depicting the encounter between the Highway Rat and the squirrel. Identify two words that suggest the squirrel's fear, ('shiver', 'shake'). Explore the illustrations for further clues (for example, his terrified facial expression). Ask: *How do you think the squirrel felt when the Highway Rat took his sack of nuts?* Invite children to write words describing these feelings on their whiteboards, such as 'frightened', 'upset', 'unhappy', 'sad', 'angry'. Share these words.

- Recall previous hot-seating activities, and discuss memorable character roles the children have undertaken. If this is a new experience, explain what is meant by a 'hot-seat'.

- Choose a child to be questioned in role as one of the animals. Invite the class to question the child about his/her feelings, encouraging them to try to follow the child's answer with a related question.

- Divide the children into eight groups with access to copies of *The Highway Rat*. Ask each group to pull a name card out of a box. They should then discuss possible questions to ask this character before one of the group takes the hot-seat. Encourage children to take turns to ask questions.

- Bring the class together and share what each group found out about their character's feelings.

Differentiation

Extension: Challenge children to think of their own words to describe each character. Get them to talk about their choice with a partner before adding them under their pictures.

6. Exploring echoes

Objective

To use spoken language to develop understanding through speculating, hypothesising, imagining and exploring ideas.

What you need

Copies of *The Highway Rat*; large plastic containers such as waste paper bins or buckets; objects to speak through such as cones, plastic pipes or cardboard tubes.

Cross-curricular link

Science

What to do

- Focus on the two spreads in *The Highway Rat* involving the cave echo.

- Read the text on the first spread and ask the children what they think is happening when the word 'sister' is repeated. Ask: *Why do the words get smaller?* (to show the sound is getting quieter) *Whose voice is coming from the cave?* Encourage children to speculate before establishing that the voice is an echo of words spoken by the characters. Discuss how the duck understands echoes and uses them to fool the rat into thinking her sister is in the cave.

- Ask the children to share past experiences of hearing their voices echoing in a tunnel, cave or large room. Explain that echoes are formed by sounds bouncing off hard surfaces, such as walls in a cave or tunnel, and travelling back again to those who are listening.

- Look together at the penultimate spread (the Highway Rat in the cave). Encourage children to imagine the conversation he might have with the bats or frogs in the 'echoey cave'. Suggest pairs role play the conversation with echoes, speaking through echo equipment such as waste paper bins, buckets and tubes.

- Bring the class together to share their role plays.

Contrasting characters

- Read the words in the boxes below.
- If the word describes the rat, colour the box red.
- If the word describes the duck, colour the box blue

clever	rude	plucky	beast
cruel	brave	baddie	adventurous
fierce	friend	rough	strong

- Draw a picture of each character in the correct box.

The Highway Rat	The duck

GET WRITING ▶

1. Questions and answers

> ### Objective
> To begin to punctuate sentences using a capital letter and a full stop, question mark or exclamation mark.
>
> ### What you need
> Photocopiable page 29 'Fascinating rat facts'.
>
> ### Cross-curricular link
> Science

What to do

- Display photocopiable page 29 'Questions and answers', and establish why it is a non-fiction sheet. Read the facts together.

- Explain that the five facts are followed by incomplete questions, and that the object of this activity is to complete each question by adding the missing punctuation and/or word/words. Revise question words and the basic punctuation rules to remember when writing questions (capital letters to begin and question marks to end each question).

- Provide individuals with the photocopiable sheet to complete. When they have finished, ask pairs to check each other's work for correct content and punctuation. Remind them that there may be more than one correct question in some cases.

- Bring the class together to discuss the answers to the questions together, focusing on how the answer should be worded and punctuated (a full stop rather than a question mark). Invite volunteers to write answers on the board.

> ### Differentiation
> **Extension:** Ask children to write their own questions relating to the following facts:
> 1. Rats make a strange noise that sounds like human laughter. 2. Rats were one of the first animals to be sent into space.

2. The Highway Rat's diary

> ### Objective
> To spell the days of the week.
>
> ### What you need
> Copies of The Highway Rat, photocopiable page 30 'The Highway Rat's diary'.

What to do

- Read The Highway Rat with the class. Choose children to write the numbers one to seven down the board and decide together the main story events to write alongside them, starting with the rat riding down the highway and ending with him working in the cake shop. Use photocopiable page 30 'The Highway Rat's diary' to identify these events (without showing the children) and make suggestions to help them if necessary.

- Speculate that the story events took place over a week and that the rat kept a diary to remind him of what happened each day. Refer to the list you made to decide what the rat might have included.

- Display the photocopiable page and explain that this is the page from the rat's diary but that some words are missing.

- Fill in the blank spaces in the first row together as an example, discussing how to spell the missing words 'Sunday' and 'highway'.

- Provide individual photocopiable sheets to complete, and copies of the book for those needing support recalling story detail.

- Divide into pairs to check one another's completed pages. Focus on the correct spelling of the days of the week, discuss reasons for errors.

> ### Differentiation
> **Support:** Provide children with the missing words for each sentence and get them to choose which sentence they should write the words in.

3. Flies, milk and hay

Objective
To sequence sentences to form short narratives.

What you need
Copies of *The Highway Rat*.

What to do
- Identify the regular pattern of language and dialogue when the Highway Rat meets the rabbit, squirrel and ants along the highway. For example, the rat always greets the animal first ('Who goes there?', 'Stand and deliver!') before demanding something he really likes, such as sweets. Inevitably the animal does not have these things but states what he/she does have. The rat always steals the food mentioned, chanting 'I am the Rat of the Highway…'

- Speculate why Julia Donaldson did not follow the same pattern with the rat's encounters with the spider, cat and horse. Draw attention to the rhyming words 'way' and 'hay' and comment that, despite the lack of dialogue, the rhyming pattern continues so that the book flows.

- Divide into six groups, allocating the spider, cat or horse equally between them. Invite each group to write a new section, based on the encounter between the allocated animal and the rat.

- Encourage the children to write in sentences that follow the discussed sequence (meeting, demanding, taking), and to include dialogue.

- Once the groups are satisfied with their writing, bring them together to read their work aloud. Decide together which group has followed the sequence discussed most accurately.

Differentiation
Support: Ask children to write only about the first part of the encounter.

Extension: Ask children to imagine the rat met another animal and write about it. Remind them to use the same pattern of language and dialogue as in the book.

4. I am sorry!

Objective
To read aloud their writing clearly enough to be heard by their peers and the teacher.

What you need
Copies of *The Highway Rat*.

Cross-curricular link
PSHE

What to do
- After reading *The Highway Rat*, focus on the final spread. Ask the children how the rat has changed since the beginning of the story. Use contextual clues, for example, his apparent dejection, and the words 'thinner', 'greyer', 'meeker', 'robs… no more'. (Explain the meaning of 'meeker' if necessary.) Discuss whether the rat has learned that it is wrong to steal, and talk about how he could make amends for his actions.

- Suggest that the rat might write letters to the animals concerned apologising for his bad behaviour, and promising he will never steal again.

- Recall a simple, informal letter format, creating an example on the board showing the layout. Revise sentence structure and punctuation rules.

- Divide into groups, asking each group member to choose one of the rat's victims and then write a letter from the rat to this victim. Suggest that they discuss the planned letter content and layout as a group first.

- Invite individuals to read their finished letters to the group, and then make any alterations in the light of the group responses.

- Swap letters with another group and ask members to take turns to read one aloud before deciding together which one most clearly demonstrates the rat's changed attitude.

- Invite the writers of the chosen favourites to read them to the whole class.

Differentiation
Support: Provide children with a framework to help them structure their letter and accept less writing.

5. What next?

Objective

To sequence sentences to form short narratives.

What you need

Copies of *The Highway Rat*; a favourite story with a sequel, such as *Zog* and *Zog and the Flying Doctors* (Julia Donaldson).

What to do

- Read the chosen book and then hold up the sequel and ask what the children think this story might be about. Read this story. Introduce the word 'sequel' and explain that a sequel follows a story, often with the same main characters in a different situation. Identify common characters in the two stories and discuss similarities and differences in events.

- Tell the children they are going to write a short sequel to *The Highway Rat*. Discuss which characters might appear and talk about events that might occur. Ask whether the children think that the rat might return to stealing or whether he is now a reformed character.

- Revise story structure, with a definite beginning, middle and end, and spend time discussing the importance of sequencing sentences so that they form short narratives.

- Recall discussions about Julia Donaldson's style and suggest that the repetition and rhyme will continue in the sequel.

- Share sequel ideas together as a class; considering options for the beginning, middle and end.

- Ask the children to write their own sequel to the story using the ideas from your discussion to help them or coming up with their own ideas.

- Divide children into pairs to read each other's sequels. Encourage individuals to share feedback.

Differentiation

Support: Focus on writing a short narrative from their sequel of at least three sentences, including an opening and closing sentence.

6. Wanted posters

Objective

To discuss what they have written with the teacher or other pupils; to write for different purposes.

What you need

Copies of *The Highway Rat*, examples of 'wanted' posters from books or the internet, large sheets of paper, art materials, individual whiteboards.

Cross-curricular links

ICT, art and design

What to do

- Read *The Highway Rat*. Recall earlier activity discussions about how the animals felt when their food was stolen. Explore the illustration of the animals' celebration after the Highway Rat had gone and describe the animals' feelings.

- Ask the children what the animals could have done if the duck had not helped them. Introduce the idea of 'wanted' posters and display some examples, discussing their purpose. Suggest creating a wanted poster to help to capture the rat.

- Allow time for groups of children to explore wanted poster images and make notes about their content on their whiteboards. Support those who need help.

- Bring the class together to discuss their findings. Make a list of appropriate poster sub-headings based on the children's notes, for example, 'Name', 'Appearance', 'Crime', 'Reward'.

- Emphasise the need to make the poster attractive to capture interest, for example, with a detailed picture of the villain and colourful border. Talk about words to include under their chosen sub-headings, for example, describing the rat's clothing and his crime. Discuss possible rewards.

- Allow groups time to create a poster, providing a wide selection of art materials and copies of the book to explore.

- Bring the class back together to present their posters and describe the content.

 # Questions and answers

● Read these facts about rats. Then add the correct punctuation or words to complete the questions.

I. Rats belong to the group of animals known as rodents.

These animals have sharp teeth and gnaw their food.

Question: What group do rats belong to _____

2. Rats' teeth keep growing throughout their lives so they chew on wood to keep them short.

Question: _____ do rats chew on?

3. Some people keep rats as pets.

They are very clever animals with good memories.

Question: _____ rats have good memories _____

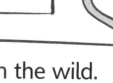

4. Rats are very sociable animals that live in groups in the wild.

A group of rats is called a 'mischief'.

Question: _____ is a group of _____

5. Male rats are called bucks, female rats are called does and baby rats are called kittens.

Question: _____ are baby _____

The Highway Rat's diary

- Write the name of a day of the week in the correct order in each small box. Then fill the blank spaces in each sentence with the missing words.

	On _____ I rode along the _____ looking for a traveller to steal from.
	On _____ I met a rabbit with a bunch of _____. I stole that.
	On _____ I met a squirrel with a sack of _____. I stole them.
	On _____ I met some ants carrying a _____. I stole that.
	On _____ I met a duck. The duck led me into a _____ and I got lost.
	On _____ I found my way out of the darkness and came out at the other side of the _____.
	On _____ I started to work in a _____ shop, sweeping the floor.

ASSESSMENT ▶

1. Revise and retell

> ### Objective
> To become very familiar with key stories and retell them.
>
> ### What you need
> Copies of *The Highway Rat*, individual whiteboards.

What to do

- Discuss stories that the children have enjoyed, and decide which genre they belong to, for example, fairy, traditional and fantasy tales, and stories with patterned language or familiar settings. Read *The Highway Rat* to the class and discuss the type of story this might be. Perhaps it fits into more than one category? (patterned language/fantasy)

- Recall guided reading sessions when the book was discussed in four separate sections. Divide the board into four and write significant events in each section to aid recall.

- Divide the class into groups of four and ask each group to retell the story to the rest of the class. To make this easier, suggest that each group member focuses on one of the four sections discussed earlier, identifies key events in their section, and writes these events on their whiteboard as a memory aid.

- Allow time for groups to practise their retelling, taking each section in order and referring to notes for support. Share as a class.

- Discuss the story telling with the class and decide together which group was the most accurate and entertaining. Assess individuals for their familiarity with the story and its particular characteristics.

> ### Differentiation
> **Support:** Focus on recalling a favourite section of the story.

2. Get to grips with grammar

> ### Objective
> To use the grammatical terminology in English Appendix 2 in discussing their writing.
>
> ### What you need
> Copies of *The Highway Rat*, copies of Extract 1.

What to do

- Display Extract 1 and read it together. Recall that it is the opening page of the story.

- Using the terminology in English Appendix 2, question the children to assess their knowledge and understanding. For example, invite children to point to a singular and plural word, a letter and a capital letter. Ask them to identify a sentence, and to find words ending with the suffixes 'ed' and 'ing'. (Use the term 'verb' if they are ready.) Search for the words 'and'/'And' used as joining words between groups of words to make sentences. Find adjectives used to describe nouns.

- Once all terminology has been revised, provide individual extract copies for children to annotate. Write instructions on the board such as: *Underline all nouns on your sheet in red. Underline all adjectives in blue. Highlight verbs ending in 'ed' and 'ing'.*

- Once the children have finished annotating their sheets, work through the displayed extract so that the children can self-assess their work.

> ### Differentiation
> **Support:** Ask children to find punctuation marks only, using the correct terminology as they talk through their work.
>
> ---
>
> **Extension:** Recall the words 'past' and 'present'. Ask: *Do you think this extract is in the past or the present? Can you change the wording so that it is in the present?*

3. Moral tales

Objective
To write sentences by re-reading what they have written to check that it makes sense.

What you need
Copies of *The Highway Rat*.

Cross-curricular link
PSHE

What to do

- Read *The Highway Rat* and recall previous discussions about whether it is wrong to steal. Talk about the consequences of the rat's stealing on the poor hungry animals.

- Encourage the children to share their own experiences of when they have had something they value taken away from them. Talk about how they felt, and what was done to make amends.

- Revise story structure by focusing on the beginning, middle and end of *The Highway Rat*. Discuss how the beginning of the story sets the scene and introduces the main character; the middle focuses on the rat's stealing and how it affects the poor animals; and the end results in a satisfactory conclusion that ensures that the rat never steals again.

- Suggest that the children write their own stories about a character who steals things. Encourage them to consider the consequences of this stealing to the character and victim/s.

- Allow time for children to plan and write their stories, emphasising the need to write in sentences and to have a clear structure. Remind them to check that their work makes sense when they have completed it and to make changes if they need to.

- Once the stories are completed, use peer assessment by inviting children to find partners to read their work, and advise where to change wording if necessary.

Differentiation
Support: Invite pairs of children to compose two or three sentences each about why they like the story. They can repeat their sentences to the class.

4. Book review

Objective
To compose a sentence orally before writing it.

What you need
Copies of *The Highway Rat*.

What to do

- Recall, or explain, the purpose of a book review, reading a few examples from familiar book covers (perhaps other Julia Donaldson books or books the class have read together). Discuss comments made about settings, characters and events and find any common features.

- Explain that you would like the children to write a review for *The Highway Rat*.

- With the earlier review discussion in mind, compile a list of headings to support the children as they write (title, setting, main character, events, illustrations and so on).

- Refresh children's memories by reading *The Highway Rat* to them with the headings you have listed still displayed. After reading, ask: *What do you think of the main character? What did you like best about the settings in this story? Was there anything you disliked? How important do you think the illustrations are? What effect do you think the rhyming words have on the story?*

- Invite the children to write their reviews in sentences, and explain that you would like them to say their sentences aloud before writing them down. Ask children to work in pairs in order to share their sentences and discuss them before writing (this will act as peer assessment).

- Allow time for the class to share and comment on the finished reviews. Ask whether children's opinions of the book have changed in the light of reviews written and heard.

Differentiation
Support: Encourage children to write a short sentence about an experience of losing something or having something of value taken away from them.